Achieve Your CRM Value? *Engage!*

By

Dean Sharratt

Copyright © 2014 by Dean F. Sharratt

All rights reserved.

ISBN-13: 9781495360305

TABLE OF CONTENTS

INTRODUCTION	vii
WHO SHOULD READ THIS BOOK?	ix
ACKNOWLEDGEMENTS:	xi
1: THE CHALLENGE OF CHANGE	**1**
1.1 Making the Case for Change	3
1.2 The Change Adoption Gap	6
1.3 Lessons Learned from Previous CRM Implementations	14
2: ESSENTIAL INGREDIENTS IN ACHIEVEMENT OF CRM VALUE	**19**
2.1 View Salespeople as Knowledge Workers and Data as Their Oxygen	21
2.2 Develop a Vision for CRM – Start with the Right Perspective!	24
2.3 Implement a Change Management Program	29
2.4 Identify Key Roles in Change Management	41
2.5 Conduct a Change Assessment - Who is "Ready" for Change?	46
2.6 Provide Coaching and Support for Adoption	49
2.7 Measure Change Adoption Progress	53
2.8 Evaluate the Role of Compensation in Achieving Change Adoption	63
2.9 Implement Overall Program Governance – *Pulling It All Together*	66
3. FRAMEWORK FOR HARVESTING CRM VALUE	**71**
Pulling It All Together	73
3.1 Vision for CRM – Start with Right Perspective, and Right People!	76
3.2 Design	79
3.3 Implement	82
3.4 Harvest the Benefits	84
SUMMARY	91
SOURCES:	95
ABOUT THE AUTHOR	99

INTRODUCTION

There is a general consensus that today's CRM* business system implementations are technically successful, but fail to deliver their expected business value. This is not surprising as the business value is predicated upon a defined change in behavior of the sales force. The real effort to achieve this change does not commence until after the technical implementation of the CRM business system has occurred (i.e., gone live) and all the project technical and project management experts have gone home. This leaves the responsibility for achieving this change adoption solely in the hands of the sales organization. This is a daunting task, one which they were generally neither expecting nor prepared for. Consequently, to realize the business value of their CRM business system implementation, sales executives must engage, prepare their organization, and lead it through the successful change in behavior that will enable this value.

The fundamental messages for sales executives are:

1. "If you want to achieve the value, then engage!"
2. The hard work starts after your CRM implementation goes live, and the responsibility for adoption success rests solely within your sales organization.
3. If you can't measure the change in the new requisite behavior, you will not achieve the ultimate benefits of your CRM business system.

Sales executive engagement in this book refers to: active participation in setting direction, allocating resources, adopting, influencing others to adopt, rewarding others for adopting, and commitment to impacting the management of

---

* Customer Relationship Management (CRM)

the CRM business system to achieve its expected business value. In effect, this embraces what great leaders already do; build infrastructure and develop capabilities that will ensure future success and growth.

This book's focus is on assisting sales executives in achieving this essential change adoption. To be successful this change must be defined and implemented within a broader business context to ensure that the necessary supporting events have occurred that can position change for success. This book describes both the required elements of this broader context, and the behavior change adoption effort, within a change program, as seen from the perspective of the sales executive.

Tracking this successful change adoption is critical to realizing the envisioned business value. The challenge for sales executives is to have the measurements in place to give them the visibility that the required change efforts are creating the desired impact on adoption of the new business process. Full adoption by all participants in the sales business process enables the specific value that the sales executives identified, and further assists them to meet their goals for the CRM business system. Once adoption takes hold, going forward executive management should insist on measuring the overall performance of their sales process to ensure that it is delivering their expected business value.

In summary, achieving the adoption of the change imposed by a new CRM business system falls solely on the sales organization. To be successful, sales executives must engage to set the goals, the direction, and create the change environment in which all sales users will adopt the new sales behavior. The sales executives must also insist that the critical change in behavior is tracked and managed as it enables their expected business value. This book describes an approach to do so.

WHO SHOULD READ THIS BOOK?

The interests of several audiences may be addressed by this book:

1. The sales executive who wants to ensure that the envisioned value of a planned new CRM business system will be realized, and who is prepared to engage with the championing and the using of the new business system following its implementation to drive the required change in sales force behavior.

2. The sales executive who has just implemented a new CRM business system and is concerned that the enabling change in behavior is not materializing.

3. The business consultant who has been successful in implementing CRM business systems and now wishes to extend services beyond implementation to assist clients through successful change adoption to realize the client's expected value of the business system.

4. Anyone who wants to get a better understanding into the context for, the challenges and the key management actions required to harvest the value of a CRM business system implementation.

5. Anyone who wants to provide an insightful resource to a decision maker who is responsible for achieving the business value of a CRM implementation.

ACKNOWLEDGEMENTS:

This book grew out of my experiences in implementing CRM solutions across several different sales organization structures over several years, within the same corporation. This was otherwise characterized by many as "same game, different players". While the implementations were technically successful, I was frustrated by the inability of each sales organization to reach the "pot of gold" described at the beginning of each implementation. After leaving, I had the time to research and discuss my experiences with others. Turns out I was not alone! So, for all of you out there with similar experiences and frustrations, I wrote this book.

The content of this book is based upon both my experiences, and the many inputs and ideas from others directly and through their published research. In particular would like to acknowledge the contribution of the following:

- Marguerite Harris for Change Management
- Serge Deschamps for results chain techniques
- Ken McLennan for sales management insights
- Dave Neal for change into smaller organizations
- Jason Whitehead for CRM business system change

In addition, I have generalized the thoughts and ideas of many who participated in several LinkedIn Discussion Groups. These discussions are always interesting, informative, and often provocative.

Finally, I would like to thank my wife and family for encouraging me to write this book. They supported me over the many years that I practiced sales, and they supported me in this journey of documenting what I learned.

1: THE CHALLENGE OF CHANGE

The challenge of change is often represented by the following sentiment - *"I am all in favor of change, you should change!"* To be successful with the introduction of change, the person represented by *"I"* must become engaged.

1.1 Making the Case for Change

A literature search reveals what many sales executives are concerned about, most CRM business system implementations are just not delivering as promised. The examples below are a few of many that are quoted throughout today's literature:

- Over 50% of CRM business system implementations fail to deliver on promised benefits. [1]
- Up to 25% of the value of a CRM business system is lost due to poor user adoption. On top of that, CRM projects fail at a rate of 50 – 70%. [2]
- CRM initiatives currently have a 63% fail rate. [3]
- An estimated 75% of new sales process implementations are not adopted by the sales force. [4]

If this was the success rate in your manufacturing production department you would likely be asking a lot of questions: do we have the right production process, the right tools, the right materials, the right standards, the right people, and the right customers? Maybe it's all of the above? If you manage an R&D group then a 50% success rate could be good performance. However, Sales is not R&D! The good news is that as a result of all these unintended R&D efforts of others, you can leverage these lessons learned to successfully harvest the benefits from improved performance of your own new CRM business system implementation.

So what are others doing as a result of this learning opportunity? The answer involves strategy, business systems and people as highlighted in following examples:

- 52 percent of sales organizations are now in the process of or planning to migrate to a new CRM system in 2013. [5]

- Many CEOs rank CRM as their most important area of investment to improve their business over the next five years. [6]
- With 70 to 80 percent of their total cost of sales tied up in personnel, sales executives must rank very highly the need to hire salespeople who fit and can be trained to excel within their organization. [7]

A big contributor to past failing experiences is a view by sales management that CRM is a tool for the salespeople. CRM is not simply a tool implementation to assist the salespeople and others. It's a business philosophy. It is a cultural change. It is a business strategy; implemented using a software solution that typically embraces the customer facing departments (e.g., sales, marketing, customer service) of your company. It is all wrapped up in a new CRM business system which imposes changes on the way your sales business is conducted, and how the work of the salespeople is conducted. Because change is so challenging, many companies just let it go.

To illustrate this challenge consider the following. The average years of experience of most salespeople and sales managers is likely measured in the 10's or 20's of years, but the average years of employment with their current firm is likely to be less than 3 to 5. All come to their current employer with a great deal of experience and prior training in how to conduct a sales pursuit. Unfortunately they are likely all different in various ways, causing difficulties in communicating progress and in delivering the necessary coaching for improved performance. A sales version of the Tower of Babel perhaps! To address this impediment the company must establish a common approach to a sales pursuit, and have all of their sales force members change their behavior to adopt this new approach. To be sure this is challenging, but essential!

The challenge is not in implementing the new CRM business system. The challenge is in bridging the gap between old and new requisite sales force behavior. This is particularly challenging when the sales organization's typical pursuit is a large, complex sales opportunity which requires several months to conclude. Without bridging this gap the organization will fail to achieve their expect value/benefits[*].

This change in behavior enables the expected benefits. The required people-side work is much different from the system implementation work (i.e. the technical-side); conducted by different people. As noted above, a new way of thinking is required to achieve the required change adoption. And as McKinsey's research shows, sales executive involvement is the essential to this success. Those organizations who master this change adoption will both realize their expected business benefits, and also develop an organizational maturity for future change that provides them with the strategic advantage of an adaptable sales force over their competitors in years to come.

> There are **two separate, but related, efforts required** to harvest the benefits of a CRM business system, as illustrated in Figure 1.1 on the next page:
>
> 1. To implement the technical solution, this is generally well known and for the most part successful today.
>
> 2. To accomplish the required change adoption, the people-side, that enables the expected benefits. This behavior change certainly has both in the past and to a large extent in the present been overlooked.

---

[*] In this book the terms "value" and "benefits" are used interchangeably.

6 The Challenge of Change

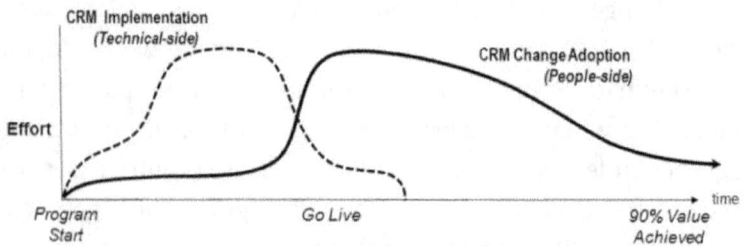

Figure 1.1 Effort-to-Value Profiles

The focus of this book is about the required change adoption, the people-side. While the book describes the actions, skills, and behavior that are critical and required to achieve adoption, it's focus is on the need to measure specific progress on a few key outcomes that indicate progress toward the required adoption. In a complex sales environment it may take several weeks, months, perhaps up to a year before clearly observable business results appear. If sales management waits that long to check for success it may be too late to take corrective action (i.e., big surprise, no benefits, game over!) Therefore, this adoption measurement is essential, commencing within weeks of implementation, and when managed, can enable the expected benefits of the new sales process several months down the road.

1.2 The Change Adoption Gap

> The challenge is not about the technical implementation, it is all about the human behavior adoption challenge, the people-side.

We have learned a great deal about the challenges of implementing business systems, particularly CRM business systems. Today, in general, the capabilities of the technology infrastructure (technology, people, content) exceed the ability of most organizations to absorb and adopt quickly.

Depending upon a sales organization's prior experience with adopting business change its challenge gap may be larger or smaller. This is illustrated in figure 1.2 below. As a sales organization develops maturity in adopting change, it can more quickly absorb the introduction of new enabling procedures and technologies.

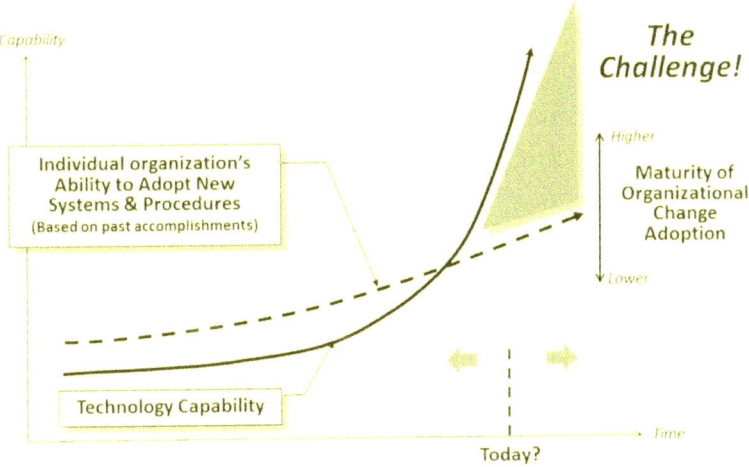

Figure 1.2 The Challenge of Adoption for a Sales Organization

On the other hand, those sales organizations that experience high sales personnel turnover generally send that maturity out the door with the turnover. They must start all over each time; as a result they never get to a level of maturity and constantly struggle to have the change adopted. They go through the same experience each time, a bit like the movie "Groundhog Day". This also brings to mind that old proverb about "Doing the same thing over and over again and expecting a different outcome is the definition of insanity".

Most of the failed CRM business system implementations focused attention primarily on the business process and information systems changes necessary to implement the new system (AKA the "CRM Project"). The focus on preparing the salespeople (i.e. people-side) was limited to communication and initial training during the implementation. While these steps are required, they are not sufficient, and the sales executives are not likely to achieve their expected benefits for the new CRM business system. Not only are they likely to fail to realize the benefits, they would also have incurred both the cost of the investment in the "technical project", and the potential loss of sales due to the disruption caused by the new business system introduction. The real focus of CRM business system implementations must be on the salespeople's adoption of the business change and associated new behaviors.

This does not imply that the approach to defining and implementing the new CRM business system is wrong. In fact, corporate and consulting organizations generally have a very workable and repeatable approach. However, the key missing ingredient to meeting the adoption gap challenge is the sales organization's focus on full adoption by all sales process participants (i.e., *people*) following implementation of the new CRM business system. This adoption effort must ramp up where today's implementation efforts are wrapping up! This is illustrated in figure 1.3 on the next page. This ramp up must address two important possible inflection points in the business value curve:

- "Implementation dip"
- "Earlier termination of value"

The *implementation dip* occurs immediately following go-live and results from the time and effort it takes for the salespeople to get trained, and become proficient in the new way of working. This takes time away from selling, hence a likely impact on sales results. A good change program can minimize the depth and duration of this impact, but not eliminate it. Sales executives should include the impact of this dip in their CRM business system plans. Note: For simplicity change is presented as a single event, in reality change is usually implemented in several releases of "adoptable" change.

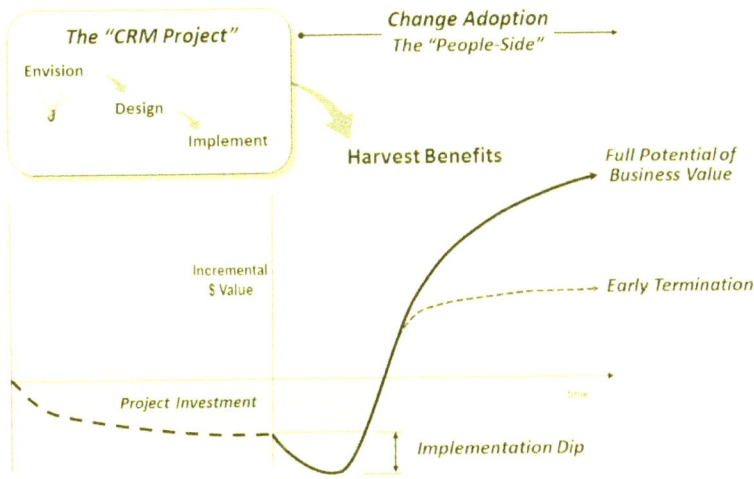

Figure 1.3 The Change Adoption Profile

The *early termination of business value* occurs when people do not fully adopt the change. Reasons for this include; how the management of the full undertaking itself changes over the timeline, and how the management of change adoption is approached. Consider the following typical scenario: The familiar front end part including implementation is typically run as a formal project, with a project manager, business and IT participants, deliverables, tasks, timetables, and with the objective of successfully turning over the new CRM business system to the user. It is seen as a very tight focused effort, those few involved from sales and other functions set aside the required time to participate, and upon completion expect to go back to their business as usual job or on to their next assignment. The work of adopting the change in behavior (i.e. harvesting the benefits), however, takes on a different complexion. It is now all about adoption of the new behaviors defined in the business change. It becomes part of the daily operation. The participants now become *all* of the people who participate in the sales business process (perhaps including some people beyond the sales organization). The achievement of success is now solely in the sales organization. The management of success now becomes diffused across all levels of the organization's sales management. Those who participated in the implementation may now be either one of the change managers, in a support role, or have moved on. The management of change adoption now gets wrapped up as part of the daily sales business of the organization with each sales manager having to make trade-off decisions about where to focus their time (e.g., selling versus change adoption). The time to full benefits realization

> **Warning:** Lookout for change adoption fatigue which can lead to early termination of value!

may not be a few weeks, but be seen as "dragging on" for perhaps several months. A real sense of weariness can set in, leading sales management to "settle" with whatever change they can get. At this point the full potential business value has failed due to earlier termination.

A different perspective of how to manage the work of change adoption during the Change Adoption (people-side) phase is required to achieve success. It is clear that this perspective must be driven by the sales executive. The key message to them is "If you want success, get engaged and stay engaged until it is realized". The good news is there is help available!

Those sales organizations who master this adoption challenge both harvest the expected benefits of their CRM business system implementation, and build the organizational maturity that enables a more rapid deployment of future change, i.e., a competitive advantage. By building this advantage these companies are positioned to move ahead of their competitors in the marketplace, substantially increasing the gulf between those who have mastered the change adoption challenge and those who have not.

> **Build a Competitive Advantage:** Those organizations who figure out how to master change adoption will not only realize value from their change, but also give themselves a strategic advantage over their competitors who have not yet done so.

The focus of discussion in various sales operations and consulting communities is now about the need to achieve this adoption of planned business system change. Recently there was an informative discussion in a LinkedIn Discussion Group; the topic was "OK, we got Salesforce. Now how do we get salespeople to REALLY use it?". It was fascinating due to both the topic and the overwhelming depth and breadth of the contributors' comments; over 100! A brief analysis revealed key messages that came through the very broad nature of this discussion. Overall, just four categories accounted for 80% of the total comments, and they were:

1. Change Adoption – 48% of comments
2. Implementation – 15%
3. Data and Reporting – 9%
4. Tools & Techniques – 8%

It was not surprising that Change and Implementation made up just over 60% of the total comments as this was the main discussion topic. However, contributors did step outside of change and implementation (40% of comments) to caution that design components also have the potential for a big impact on adoption.

Since Change Adoption made up almost 50% of the comments overall, this category was further broken down to dominant key change messages. Of this subset just five change topics accounted for 60%, they were:

1. Communicate the value of CRM to Salespeople – 15%
2. Sales Management provides coaching to Salespeople on both process and content – 12%
3. Sales Management's active participation required – 12%
4. Use Formal Change Management Program to achieve Adoption – 11%
5. Use carrot approach to incent Salespeople – 7% (Using a Stick approach contributed a further 4%)

Those familiar with implementing change adoption programs may recognize that all five of these topics are typically part of a change program in some fashion (with one specifically directed at a change program).

This discussion reinforced the need for a formal CRM change adoption program (also referred to as change management), where the above five topics are some (but perhaps not all) of the necessary ingredients for success. Readers should also be mindful that successful adoption is enabled by a relevant design for a specific organization.

In summary, to harvest the benefits of their new CRM business system sales organizations must achieve adoption of their new business system. A formal change adoption program is required to bridge the behavioral gap (i.e., people-side component) between the old and the new sales business system. While the nature of the technical-side effort to envision, design, and implement the new CRM business system is well known and visible, the nature of the change adoption program (i.e. the people-side) to harvest the expected business value/benefits is less evident. Both are required; the focus for sales management should now be on the CRM change adoption aspect. Successful change adoption will increase the envisioned business benefits and value (i.e., greater ROI) of the business system implementation. To be successful, sales organizations must master both of these aspects of their CRM business system endeavor. Those organizations who figure out how to master change adoption will also give themselves a strategic advantage over their competitors who have not yet done so. To achieve this success will require fresh thinking at the sales executive and management levels; the opportunity is there, but *if management wants it they will have to engage and live the change!*

1.3 Lessons Learned from Previous CRM Implementations

A search through the literature and personal experience resulted in the following list of lessons learned from previous CRM business systems implementations. Since most readers will recognize these quickly they are presented in bullet form.

- Sales management involvement missing - a key participant
- CRM vision not fully defined:
    - CRM business system implementation not approached from business perspective.
    - CRM business system is seen successful when just the technology goes live.
    - CRM business system put in place to police salespeople.
    - CRM business system was sold and implemented to serve management's needs, salesperson's needs treated as an afterthought (i.e., needs to create value for the sale people as well as management).
    - Customer experience is not defined.
- Common Design Issues:
    - System designed to capture too much data; burden on salespeople (i.e., ease of use).
    - Sales managers and top performing salespeople not included in business system and CRM technology design development.
    - Assumption that one process fits all types of sales opportunities; some sales organizations may sell both simple and complex solutions.
    - Sales business process and sales opportunity pipeline stages within technology must align.

- o Electronic system must support convenient access by all device types (PC, smart phone, tablet, ..) used by salespeople.
- Implementation Issues:
  - o A "build it and they will come" mentality prevails toward change adoption.
  - o Sales managers not provided training on how to coach for change adoption.
  - o Architects and implementers of new CRM business system must have a solid, well thought out architecture that can be implemented in phases in a way that new functionality has minimal impact on that which was previously delivered. Changes to existing functionality should be primarily to fix errors or improve the experience based on field input.
  - o Several cycles of changes to what has previously been implemented leads to situations where the salespeople eventually take the position "I think I will sit this round out!"
- Post-implementation Issues:
  - o Salespeople do not use the new system, or only partially, and not consistently.
  - o Initial adoption started but not reinforced, sales users fall back to old habits.
  - o Insufficient support, both in amount and kind, to respond to issues and unforeseen post go-live challenges impedes adoption by sales users.
  - o Sales executives don't personally use the CRM business system to find their desired information and resort to calling salespeople, or asking for reports not produced from the new system. Consequently salespeople

- interrupted by too many calls from senior managers seeking data that was already in the new CRM.
- Executives and senior managers can't talk with salespeople in the language of the CRM business system consequently leading to confusion, misunderstanding, and frustration, creating a new "tower of babel".
- Sales managers and salespeople do not like their sales activities being monitored or reported upon. This is a challenge for change management. Reporting should be seen as a form of efficient communication not a path to punishment. Reporting should be very tightly focused on those few elements that were determined to be critical to sales deal progress and success. These elements should be the basis for effective coaching.
- Sales managers do not have the skills to coach salespeople on behavior required in new business system. Developing effective coaching skills in the sales managers is a critical part of the implementation training, and on-going training and monitoring.
- Sales managers do not have the skills, knowledge, and experience to lead the change from old to new CRM business system. Sales manager assessments will be critical to deciding who will be on the new team going forward.
- Sales managers do not invest time in learning and coaching on new CRM business system (or do not have time available). Sales executives must ensure this learning time is provided for in their implementation plans, sales managers who do not take advantage of it become a discipline issue.
- Sales manager's role in achieving adoption by salespeople overlooked or not emphasized by planners

of the new CRM business system implementation. Sales managers are the first line of coaching, while they may get coaching personally on how to coach, they must coach their own salespeople.
- Users have no confidence in the data either of the initially loaded data (part of implementation), or data gathered during operation.
- No approach and metrics defined to measure adoption; as one commenter pointed out "failure is a slow burn with big surprise at the end".
- No provision made in salespeople's workload to accommodate the added effort to learn and master the new behavior.
- Other organization changes (in Sales or other organization departments) post-implementation impact adoption of new CRM business system (i.e. change saturation).
- Performance metrics that sales management selected don't flow naturally from sales activity at field level; becomes an extra burden on salespeople.
- Sales users and others don't accept that the change will benefit them, and therefore don't change. The "what's in it for me" must be addressed, or "sold" to salespeople as part of on-going communication from beginning of developing the solution well through into operation.
- New sales managers and salespeople hired during and post implementation not given in-depth training. Part of the cost of failures by individual salespeople lies with the company's leadership because they brought people onboard, but not trained them.

- Business process not kept current, some sales activities may have been put in place to address specific crisis that has long since passed.
- Sufficient support resources not available to sustain user adoption over the life of the system.

2: ESSENTIAL INGREDIENTS IN ACHIEVEMENT OF CRM VALUE

The focus of this book is on those change actions essential for successful adoption of the new sales behavior, the people-side, which can enable management's expected business value. As discussed earlier, the actions required to successfully implement the technical solution, including business process, sales methodology, CRM software, etc., are well known and essential, and therefore covered lightly. This section focuses on those areas of thinking and actions where sales executive involvement and management can lead to this successful change adoption.

2.1 View Salespeople as Knowledge Workers and Data as Their Oxygen

It is important to reflect upon the nature of sales work when thinking about sales enablement actions (the processes, methodologies, and technologies) that may be effective in helping the sales users achieve their goals. Salespeople and sales managers are knowledge workers. They rely on the data they collect (or data otherwise available to them) to make informed decisions about what next actions to take in their sales pursuits (a bit like a doctor uses data acquired through one or more tests to diagnose a patient's illness and prescribe a course of treatment).

Sales work is different than transaction processing work where the next activities are largely predetermined by the automated business process that the worker uses. The salesperson proceeds through their journey of discovery acquiring more data about their sales opportunity, where each iteration drives them to the next appropriate actions, until the "truth" is self-evident to the client, or the salesperson concludes that conditions for success are not present and abandons or suspends the opportunity; hopefully earlier not later.

> **Perfect knowledge is a great enabler!** It's all about the value of data for the knowledge worker; this should be the focus of sales enablement.

Some vendors tell salespeople "Just follow this methodology and you will be wildly successful". The problem with this statement is that salespeople live in a world where the next action is determined by the data they just acquired and analyzed. The sales world is not something to which a highly scripted rigid process can be applied; salespeople will not rigidly follow a locked "step 1, step 2, etc." methodology. Salespeople need the flexibility to analyze the data for a particular situation, and "branch" down a different path to a common outcome. The salesperson is, in effect, reversing the above vendor's statement; they acquire the data, analyze what it tells them, and then they use a method/process to plan and accomplish the next action. No, it is not a random walk; the salesperson is expected to follow an overall opportunity management process, for example, which describes expected outcomes at various points or stages.

The salesperson must know the value of this data, particularly how it will help them to take next actions to move closer to perfect information. This is where process, methodologies, pursuit plans, training, coaching, and systems play a role. These items help to standardize both the kinds of data and its collection across a specific sales organization (i.e., incorporating best practices).

The above items standardize the language of discussion between the salesperson and sales manager; and they make data acquired accessible to all who need to know. But, avoid the trap of focusing on these activities alone; keep the primary focus on the data.

If the salesperson does not know why and how to collect the data and what to do with it, they will see little value in it and resist collecting and using it. For example, if salesperson does not understand the reason for a well-qualified opportunity before proceeding into developing a proposal then all the process and data in the world will not help. Specifically, if they do not understand the need to identify a Client Coach they will likely not do it, or simply find one, check the box, and never go back to that person again.

If salespeople do not understand the need for the data they will not use it; adoption of the desired change will be aborted early. Therefore, an aspect of adoption of the new business change is ensuring that the salespeople develop this understanding of data use. The initial focus on achieving successful adoption has to be making this connection for the salesperson. A key question all planners should ask themselves is "If you cannot find value for the salesperson in the data that you are asking them to collect, then why are you asking them to collect it?"

> **Information is Key:** Successful salespeople understand why it is important to acquire certain data about a sales opportunity, and what action to take based on what they learned.

To carry this off, sales leadership must first focus on changes to the *"why"* part of their salesperson's and manager's acquisition and use of data to make decisions about their next actions (the *"what"* part), then the processes and guidelines they use (the *"how"* part) to manage this data and their business, and finally how technology could enable use of this data. (A key ingredient to successful change adoption is effective sales manager coaching, but more on that later!) If all this is "wired up" correctly then the CRM business system is seen by the salespeople as an aid not an obstacle. The focus of adoption becomes developing an understanding of and proficiency in its use, not avoiding punitive action. The value to the sales organization is in the effective use of their data together with adoption of process and methods to make better decisions which drive improved business results.

In summary, building knowledge and competence in the acquisition and use of certain key data about a sales pursuit is essential to a salesperson's adoption of the planned business change, and their success ultimately enables the sales executive's vision of improved sales performance. Salespeople should be expected to understand the fundamentals behind using this data. Sales managers are expected to coach their salespeople on this point. Clean, credible, accessible data enables salesperson adoption of the desired change. Do not burden the salespeople with too much data. They should only be expected to collect and use that which helps them to advance their sales opportunity. Salesperson's success drives adoption, which then drives sales executive's goals.

2.2 Develop a Vision for CRM – Start with the Right Perspective!

> **A Perspective of CRM:** CRM is not a product that can be purchased. It is a disciplined, integrated approach to managing relationships with customers that requires continuous improvement. It is a strategy to improve customer orientation, not a tactic, and although supported by IT, it involves considerable organizational re-design, including changing the mindsets and behaviors of managers and employees of the organization. [8]

Unsuccessful attempts at sales enablement were described in Section 1 where many sales organizations took too narrow a view of CRM and simply saw it as a tool implementation. To achieve success organizations must take a broader perspective.

Consider this perspective when setting a vision for your CRM. In this book the combination of business strategy, process, methods, and imbedded CRM technology will be referred to as CRM business system or just CRM. Running a successful small or large business requires great leaders, disciplines, methods, tools, techniques, and, most importantly, people who are motivated to contribute to the vision of the company. Management must drive vision down into the organization and translate it into something that the individual salesperson and other employees can relate to, and buy into (e.g., goals, objectives, and strategies, with linked departmental and individual targets (e.g., quotas)). There has been much written on this, likely much to come. Management must describe:

- The sales business that they are in, its strategies, functions and processes. Often this can involve organizational redesign.
- The sales business components, and how each are expected to interact with each other and with external participants (clients, suppliers, partners, etc.).
- The data required to perform the business.
- The sales methods, management guidelines (i.e., rules), and techniques used to perform successfully.
- The tools and technology to support all this.
- The internal people participants in these processes. Some of these participants (e.g., Marketing, Engineering, Delivery, Accounting, etc.) may extend beyond the sales organization which brings another aspect of complexity to successful adoption.

Through this business definition, management establishes the culture of their organization. Throughout this definition process leaders should seek input from customers, outside subject matter experts, and other thought provoking people. All of the above must come together in a balanced fashion to accomplish the purpose of their vision. The CRM business system vision can empower all the participants with a solid context that puts their various business issues into perspective, and leads them to their own conclusions about why they should care.

A new CRM sales business system is an example of such a change. One component of the overall sales business function is the sales opportunity management process. This process should define the major "stages" in the lifecycle of a sales opportunity pursuit, from initial identification, through turnover of the signed contract to the fulfillment process. It should define certain management-defined decision points that take place during each stage which require sales management (and perhaps others) approval before the opportunity proceeds. The data acquired up to that point must support this decision.

Inside each stage there is a role for sales methodology, techniques, and management guidelines to assist the salesperson to understand not only the need for, how, and from whom to acquire this data, but also what to do with the data – all those good things that a knowledgeable sales manager needs in order to coach effectively! This is where well recognized sales methodologies can play an important role in standardizing why and how management wishes their salespeople to acquire/use data as

> Just a note; this book is not about the attributes of a good opportunity management process, but, if it were, one key piece of advice would be "Don't over complicate it!"

they proceed along their journey within the context of the sales opportunity management process.

CRM vision contributes to another important business tool, the business case for implementing a new CRM business system. The business case is dependent upon a clear understanding of the proposed CRM business system goals and the expected value/benefits. These value/benefits are usually only expressed at a general level sufficient for executive approval of the proposed CRM business system. These benefits are usually predicated upon the successful implementation of certain changes in how the sales business operates that necessitates new behavior on part of the sales force. The vision of these benefits must include a recognition of and provision for the change effort to:

- Minimize the implementation dip which may occur immediately following go live, and,
- Negate early termination of business value.

In order to manage successful adoption of these changes, a linkage is required between the benefits at the company level down to those at the individual sales manager and salesperson level. If sales managers and salespeople do not adopt the requisite changes in new behavior, then the CRM business system implementation will not fully deliver the value/benefits outcomes as described in the business case.

Fortunately there are business techniques to assist management in making this linkage between benefits and adoption. The field of Benefits Management provides a technique called Results Chain [9] or Results Network [10] which can be used to establish this critical linkage of outcomes with adoption. Starting with defining their vision and continuing into subsequent phases of implementation the sales executives and managers, through a series of discussions, define a chain of events from cause to outcome (value) of their proposed CRM business system.

Included in this results chain are identified key assumptions about sale force adoption (i.e., changes in behavior), process, and technology required to enable the expected value/benefit. As an example, it is likely that one of these assumptions will deal with the need to train and coach salespeople on why, what and how to use this new data about their sales opportunities when planning their next actions. This training and coaching must be part of the plan to achieve adoption.

Once these results chain discussions identify how to measure this adoption, then change and value are linked. This results chain can illustrate the contribution of people-side adoption to the overall business value, or ROI, of the proposed CRM system. This change-value linkage is a basis for essential on-going measurement of the adoption of change. When management is able to track progress toward the adoption of change the benefits are much more likely to be achieved.

> **Linking Value to New Behavior:** When management is able to track progress toward adoption of change, benefits are much more likely to be achieved.

In summary, a broad perspective vision focuses sales executives and management on defining both change in terms of why and how data should be used by salespeople, sales managers and others in their organization, and the resulting business value – the benefits!

This vision:

- Enables a rationale for salespeople in adopting change,
- Provides a basis for training and coaching that is more business data and business process focused.
- Leads to the requirements definition of the new CRM business system.

Finally, the business case component of vision defines management's expected value, and through a Results Chain the causes of this value are identified along with assumptions about adoption of the required change. This linkage provides both the critical connection between value and adoption, and select key metrics that sales executives can use to manage change adoption's progress which enables their benefits.

2.3 Implement a Change Management Program

> **Change management** is an approach to transitioning individuals, teams, and organizations to a desired future state. Change management uses basic structures and tools to control organizational change efforts, with the goal of maximizing benefits and minimizing negative impact on those affected. [11]

When sales executives are looking at their vision for business value enabled by the implementation of a new CRM business system, it almost always involves a change in the business, the business process, technology, and new behavior for the salespeople. The value they are seeking is in achieving the full adoption of the change, not implementing the CRM business system. If the intended users (e.g., salespeople, sales managers, sales executives, and people in other organizations) don't buy into this change and adopt the requisite behavior, then the implementation will have failed to deliver its value! *Change management* programs are intended to win this buy-in.

Sales executives are aware of the role and need for project management for a CRM business system implementation. (Project management's role is to build and successfully turn over the new CRM business system to sales management.) They need no convincing that such a role is required.

The role of change management is to successfully achieve full adoption of the new business system. This role and the need for change management has only emerged in recent years as business systems have been implemented, particularly those which impact how a large number of business people work. Past implementations of CRM business systems illustrate this point. Through the lessons learned from such implementations there is a significant and growing body of knowledge in this discipline of change management. Like project management, this change management discipline may already be available inside a sales organization's company, and if not, certainly through outside consulting services.

For those sales executives questioning if they really need a change program for their CRM implementation, a few simple assessment tests might provide helpful in assessing the need for change management. The simple scorecard in figure 2.1, on the next page, could be used to quickly get a sense of the scope of change adoption for a proposed new CRM business system. Using this scorecard a sales executive could assess the contribution that change management could have on realizing the business value of a new CRM business system.

Alternatively, it could be used to consider the risk to the project benefits if change management not engaged. It is easy to use. For each of the Change Factors[12] presented, simply assess each for your proposed CRM system using the 1 – 5 scale, then total up the values for each cell selected. The minimum score is 6, and the maximum is 30.

Change Assessment Scorecard			
Change Factors	Min	Your Score each Change Factor	Max
Number of sales people impacted	Few		Many/All
Aspects of work impacted	Few		Many/All
Number of locations	Single		Many/All
Departure from current state	Small		Large
Nature of change	Incremental		Disruptive
Familiarity to sales people	Familiar		Vastly Different
Sum of Score Values for each selected Change Factor			

Figure 2.1 Change Assessment Scorecard

If the Sum of Score Values is above 20, then consider the contribution of change management to be high in achieving the requisite adoption of new behavior, and therefore critical to achieving the expected business value.

Caution: When planning your implementation, if the score is all 5's across the board then perhaps too much change is being attempted at one time. Consider ways to reduce the amount of change per implementation; a successful approach used by others includes several releases of change, each building on a growing maturity for adopting change.

Another way to use this scorecard is to score, then ask the question "If we don't invest in change management, is the risk to achieving the expected business system value increased?" One last point on the scorecard, some organizations may have a different set of change factors which are important to them based on their experience with introducing successful change.

Change management helps overcome natural resistance to change. No matter how bad the old system is, most sales force participants will have resolved themselves to a level of comfort with it and will have found all kinds of interesting workarounds for its short comings. Change programs are required to move them out of this comfort zone into the new target zone and to keep them in the new zone until it becomes the new normal zone (and seen as much better than where they were previously). Consider the following points when developing change programs:

- Salespeople view training as an imposition on reaching sales goals, "I have no time!".
- Repeat the business case for CRM business system frequently.
    - Salespeople at all levels need to understand "what's in it for me?"
    - Individualize the message for each type of sales participant, be specific.
    - Reinforce the principle that adoption of the new behavior is a personal responsibility at all levels within the organization.
- Create training plans to provide only critical training before "go-live", with the remainder parceled out in increments after "go-live". Salespeople learn by doing. All training sessions should be recorded and available for replay at salesperson's convenience for those who missed the session, a point covered in a session, or a refresher.
- Implement coaching programs to support all levels of business system users.

Essential Ingredients in Achievement of CRM Value

- Provide "hot Line" support to sales users following go-live to quickly address any issues they may have encountered in adopting new CRM business system.

- Make it easy for sales users to get additional instructions for automated systems; include instructions, information, tips on-line, in-line with the automated task sales user is attempting to perform.

- Track, manage, and make visible to all progress toward adoption of the new sales behavior.

- Provide incentives for early adoption.

Change management includes targeted communication programs that engage, not merely inform, to promote awareness and excitement about the change. The communications message should be targeted to the appropriate participant. If the message is intended for salespeople then the content should be focused on items that will engage and energized the salespeople. Programs must engage not just the "change ready" but the "change resistance"; the latter are the group that will be most problematic for successful adoption of change.

Change management must go beyond just communications and training. It must address the way in which the organization embraces and operationalizes the requisite change.

> **Nurture Adoption:** Salespeople will be asked to do new things in new ways. They need to get to a level of trust in the sales organization so that when they try something new and don't succeed the first time they will not be penalized.

Participants will be asked to do new things in new ways. They need to get to a level of trust in the organization so that when they try something new and don't succeed the first time they will not be penalized (this is where sales management's understanding of the implementation dip plays a role). All must be open to others who reach out as part of a new collaborative team. Executive management can foster this change by rewarding both those who show leadership for change wherever it occurs, and those who have achieved change.

It is important to keep in mind that change adoption is realized in increments over time as users develop proficiency and enhance their new behavior; some develop early and fast, others may take a more "wait and see" attitude. Adults learn by doing and mastering, then moving to the next increment of change. A good practice is to provide a release of change (i.e., new functionality/capability) then let salespeople and others adopt it to gain a level of proficiency, and then introduce another release. It may take several months or a year beyond the initial "go-live' date to achieve full implementation and sales user adoption. This would all be done within the context of program management which brings all of the change elements together.

Nothing is static beyond the initial change. Sales organizations evolve over time. A focus on change adoption and harvesting of expected benefits must be on-going over the life of the CRM business system. Change management and overall program management must be tightly linked to successfully coordinate operational and sales user change.

Ongoing change, monitoring, and adjustment of the implemented CRM business system solutions are important steps in sustaining organizational change. Too often, sales management focuses on the challenges of new CRM business system's initial implementation and fail to keep managing its adoption after initial installation is complete; this unfortunate behavior is referred to as "Once and done!". Absent on-going management sponsorship situations arise which can cause an early end to adoption, i.e., early termination of business value. Sales users make

> **Not a Once-and-Done Effort!** Nothing is static beyond the initial change. Sales organizations evolve over time. A focus on change adoption and harvesting of expected benefits must be on-going over the life of the CRM business system.

an initial effort to change, but change is hard and when they perceive a lack of interest by management they slide back to their old behavior.

Many sales organizations have a significant employee turnover rate. New hires at all levels, who come into the sales organization with different ideas about selling than defined by the executives' view of CRM business system, can cause conflict and confusion with the new CRM business system and weaken its adoption. Yes, there is value to bringing new proven ideas into CRM business system, in a managed fashion. Change management must define how new hire behavior will be aligned to the company position to avoid a "dilution" of the new CRM DNA and subsequent loss of the sales organization's change maturity capability.

Introducing change can create an inevitable implementation dip as illustrated earlier. Salespeople are competent and confident with what they already know. Until they reach that same point with the new business system, they won't be as productive. Provide them with the knowledge, skills, and coaching to minimize the dip. Plan for the "dip" – adjust expectations for sales results – reward/reinforce adoption.

Change management can shorten its duration and can lessen the impact of this dip, but not completely eliminate it.

A key to successful change management is *making success visible at the individual level!* On a quarterly, semiannual or annual (fiscal year) basis sales management should benchmark and promote CRM business system success in meeting their expectations set forth in their ROI statement and results chain.

> **Recognize Adoption Achievement:** Make success visible at individual level!

Reporting on these benchmarks and setting periodic "sprints" to address issues will help keep everyone engaged in the initiative and focused on the target value/benefits.

Fujitsu's Macroscope[9] points out that to succeed in delivering sales executives' expected benefits, the change programs must continually verify that the desired business results are still a priority, that initial assumptions are still valid, and also determine if adjustments are required in the priority or sequencing of efforts within the change program.

Successful change programs share a common ingredient, key people roles. A September, 2013 LinkedIn Discussion[13] supports the need for such key ingredients within a change program. A member started a very interesting discussion titled "Some sales research organizations indicate that a very small percentage of sales training provides any lasting increase in sales volume." Over 80 members responded, identifying one or more ingredients that they believe are required to make sales training "sticky" (to borrow this phrase from contributing member).

Analysis of these member responses revealed seven significant contributors (see figure 2.2, below) that were believed to have a positive impact on training stickiness. (Members identified these items in their discussion contributions). The first four of these described the desired roles of people in the sales

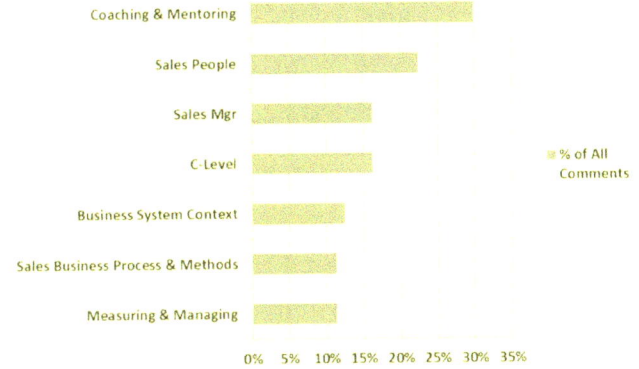

Figure 2.2 Contributors to Training "Stickiness"

organization and the key actions of these people. These four are described in more detail.

Coaching and mentoring comments focused primarily on salespeople, but several members pointed out the need to train and coach sales managers on how to coach effectively. Coaching is seen as required to achieve the salespersons' adoption of new selling behavior. Members pointed out that like all newly acquired skills, repetition and coaching is required to master the new behavior. Sales management discipline is required to ensure that effective coaching, mentoring, and follow-up with the salespeople actually occurs.

Salesperson related comments were focused on the need for coaching, mentoring, and reinforcement. The most significant personal attributes for salesperson were seen as:

- Adopting the change
- Being open to change

Most frequently used phrases associated with the salesperson were (in order of frequency):

- Change adoption
- Achieved incrementally
- Continuous process
- Allow time to change
- Learn from organization's success
- Requires repetition to master the new behavior"

Sales managers were seen as essential for coaching and mentoring their salespeople on the sales behavior change, and reinforcing them to adopt the requisite new sales behavior. Several members commented on the need to train and coach sales managers how to coach effectively. Several commented that sales manager tracking and measuring of change in salesperson's behavior was essential to successful adoption. Phrases most frequently used to describe sales manager were:

- Involved/engaged
- Has coaching skills
- Tracks progress"

C-Level involvement was seen as critical to driving the training program "top down", consistent with company goals. Phrases most frequently used to describe C-Level were:

- Involved
- Initiates the change program
- Has the right expectations about the program
- Works to get the buy-in"

Members described a training program that could be "sticky" when focused on change adoption of new sales behavior and attitudes, achieved through:

- An incremental training program driven top-down from C-level.
- Provided on continuous, just-in-time basis (not once and done).
- Where the program is aligned with company goals.
- Training change messages are reinforced by on-going sales manager coaching and mentoring.

In addition, members highlighted several key ingredients required to operationalize the successful end results of sticky training, these included:

- A business context of essential building blocks (i.e., business strategy, business process & methods, tools & techniques, management processes) within which the training program unfolds.
- Involvement of key people including C-level who have both the appropriate expectations for the program, and drive it.

- Sales managers who become effective coaches, and are disciplined in following through to ensure change is adopted as planned.

- Salespeople who are both open to change and in fact adopt the new sales behavior.

- Measurement and management of progress toward change adoption.

All the above taking place continuously, over a period of time. Overall, if training is delivered within the presence of such a change program, it will be "sticky", and the organization will realize the sales business outcomes it set out to achieve.

In summary, change management is the way by which the sales executives' vision for improved sales effectiveness is turned into a reality. Change management is the enabler for a successful people-side outcome in the overall CRM business system implementation. The connections made between the vision and the value of new salesperson behavior enables this benefits realization. Change programs are required to ensure that the sales organization successfully transitions to the expected new behavior. Getting people within a sales organization to a new level of behavior and performance is not a short term undertaking. Sales executives should have the expectation that an on-going change program must be in place and actively managed until such time that their expected benefits are fully realized. Depending upon the size and nature of the organization, this could take from several months to one (or more) years.

2.4 Identify Key Roles in Change Management

The lessons learned from many implementations are that, while the salespeople are important to overall success, the sales executives and managers carried the critical success roles. It is not sufficient for the sales management to simply "build it". They must be actively engaged in the program throughout its life through "Do" and "Reinforcement" actions.

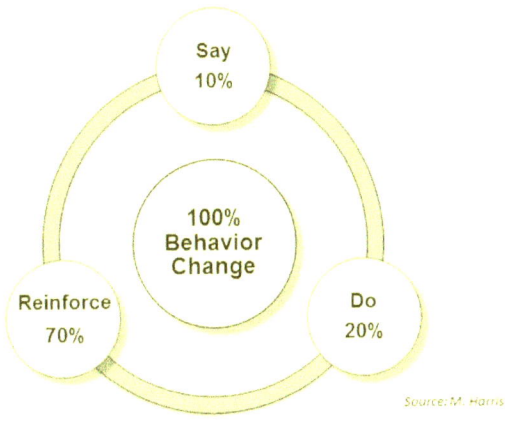

To help the organization "stay the course" leaders must be consistent in actions and "walk the talk". Leadership alignment leads to a greater degree of trust and confidence in team during a complex, lengthy implementation.

Figure 2.3 Three Leadership Actions to Accelerate Adoption

In the past most organizations viewed CRM business system implementations from the perspective of "If you build it they will come!" Unfortunately this point is also coupled with many sales managers/executives and operations types who take the position "We have spent a lot of money on this tool for the salespeople and they darn well will use it!" (Another version of "The beating will continue until morale improves.") In general, experience indicates this approach does not have a lasting improvement on behavior. If management's focus is on compliance then it will likely waste management time and potentially damage the manager-salesperson relationship.

Sales management time must be focused on:
- Coaching salespeople in adopting the desired new behavior
- Reinforcing the "early adopters"
- Rewarding the new behavior
- Providing consequences for no "new" behavior or lack of action

By allowing the status quo to continue unchecked, sales management indicates it is not serious about the "new behaviors"; salespeople read this sign, and they abandon change adoption, i.e., early termination occurs. Key aspects of these sales management roles are covered in the following paragraphs.

Sales Executive's Role

To get change adoption sales executives must be seen as actively engaged participants in the change and not bystanders, or simply just involved. They must be able to describe to the sales users both the intended change and the value that they should expect to receive when they adopt the change.

Specifically the sales executive must engage to:
- Sponsor and champion the success of the CRM business system, including allocating the required resources.
- Set the vision and expectations for the CRM business system, with emphasis on how value will flow

immediately following implementation to full adoption of the requisite change.

- Hold people accountable and insist on measureable results.
- Use the CRM business system themselves; use the terms and the data.
- Reward both change leadership and achievement of the new behaviors.
- "See it through" and insist on continuous improvement to achieve and exceed goals of sales process; In other words: which is, build infrastructure and develop capabilities that will ensure future success and growth.

Sales Manager's Role

Specifically sales management's (at all levels) full, active support and engagement throughout is essential to the success of the change adoption that enables benefits harvesting. Sales management must learn to "walk the talk". They must become active participants. Sales management must go beyond some of the prior "Do what I say" practices. They must become actively engaged in the process of change, with a major focus on reinforcing the "good" behavior that leads to adoption of their desired change.

Sales managers are vital participants in the implementation of change. They are change agents who transform executive management's vision into a practical reality in the field. They will coach each salesperson on the new business process (the target) as defined and approved by executive management so that each can master the behavior defined by the new business process. The sales managers must be positioned to say what the executive visionaries would say about the nature and value of the change when the visionaries were not there to personally say it to the salespeople. The sales managers must be enabled with the means to obtain the appropriate data to help them to both reinforce the value of the change, and to coach their salespeople effectively.

Change adoption by all levels of people who participate in the sales business process is important, but the sales managers are critical to change success. The challenge presented by the first line sales managers is - there they sit – in the middle of the road (figuratively speaking). It is hard to get around them, over them, or through them. They cannot be ignored! See quote from 2012 HBR article below.

> **"To Build a Great Team, You Need a Great Manager"** - **2012 HBR**
>
> "A team of excellent salespeople will win sales and make this year's goal, regardless of who the manager is. But the success of that team will be short lived. Eventually, an average manager will bring all of the salespeople that he manages down to his level. On the other hand, an excellent manager will bring excellence to all her territories. An excellent manager may inherit average salespeople, but in the long run she will counsel, coach, motivate, or replace salespeople until the entire team is excellent."

An organization's change adoption programs must get through to all of these sales managers (with training and other winning hearts and minds programs). The sales managers must be trained and become proficient on both the new process as well as effective coaching. The dilemma posed for the senior sales management, who own the program, is whether average (and below average) sales managers, particularly those who show little or no support for the expected change, should be moved to the side of the road before the implementation gets underway (implies some potential turnover or reassignment).

In the short term, sales management should have the understanding and expectation that post implementation of a major change in business process there will be a dip in business performance followed by an expected measurable improvement over pre-change performance. If, after the expected dip period, a positive impact of a particular sales manager's coaching is not seen, then perhaps the issue is with the sales manager. This could indicate that this manager needs attention and coaching. In the short term there is a risk that less effective managers may panic when personal compensation falls, and as a result return to their old habits, thus hobbling or terminating the full potential of the change initiative. In the long term the reward for sales management would be the increased performance of the manager's sales team. This is where executive sales management must monitor progress and step in and take corrective action when necessary.

In summary, the success of the new CRM business system is driven by the sales executives and sales managers. Yes, the salespeople and others are also participants. They must adopt the new process and become proficient in the use of the new process, tools, and techniques. But it is sales management at all levels who must engage, take ownership for, and drive the overall program through coaching and personal involvement to ensure that their expected benefits are achieved.

2.5 Conduct a Change Assessment - Who is "Ready" for Change?

Clearly, realizing the benefits of a new CRM business system is not a "build it and they will come" proposition. An assessment of the readiness of all the participants in the organization to embrace adoption of the planned change is critical to its success. This assessment will drive communications, training, initial coaching, and yes, staffing plans. Dealing with change can have consequences at both the sales manager and salesperson level, including some planned, expected, and unexpected turnover or reassignment.

> **Change Assessment** informs senior sales management of the challenges ahead!

There is an old saying that applies when successfully implementing a new CRM business system; it goes along the lines of "The teacher shall appear when the student is ready". So it follows that any CRM implementation must be accompanied with a realistic assessment of the readiness for change in the impacted parts of the organization. And to take quotes to the next level, in order to avoid the situation where some say "I am all in favor of change, the salespeople need to change" the assessment needs to include sales executives and sales management as well, particularly first line sales managers.

This change assessment must be conducted throughout the life of the CRM business system; initially during the planning, design and implementation in order to get the appropriate staffing, training, and communication programs in place, and later during the intense change period following implementation to assist or otherwise deal with those (at all levels) who are having difficulty with or resisting adoption of the change.

The scope of a full change assessment includes several elements. For example, Fujitsu's Macroscope describes the scope as:

- Provide a detailed description of the change
    o Using the BTOPP (Business Strategy, Technology, Organization, People and Process) model for structure
- Describe the impacts of the proposed improvement on the organization
- Identify risks and constraints
- Assess the change burden
- Assess change capability

However, for the purpose of this discussion, the focus will be on the people aspects of the adoption of the change imposed by the new CRM business system.

The outcome of this assessment should be a practical, realistic understanding of the impact of the proposed business change on the sales participants in the organization and their readiness to adopt this change. The assessment should yield an understanding of readiness at each level in the organization, down to the individual level. This could include an assessment of a salesperson's readiness for change along the lines of:

- Early adopter
- Follower
- Late adopter, and even
- Not suitable

The sales organization must develop or adopt training and initial coaching programs to support moving each participant (sales managers, salespeople, and others) through the change adoption curve; helping the salespeople and the sales manager toward the same change goal. But ultimately the sales manager must embrace the change and start coaching to adoption of the new business process or change adoption and benefits realization is prematurely terminated.

The reality of introducing change into an organization is that some participants are just not going to perform well in the new envisioned world. In general it is better to deal with any planned turnover prior to implementation, particularly at the critical first line sales manager level. Turnover at this level following implementation can be very disruptive to the change adoption progress. Bringing in a new manager as a replacement or net additional hire requires careful selection to ensure that the candidate will "add to" the new process environment that sales management is working to create. Bringing in a new manager who is not supportive or in alignment with this new environment will change its "DNA", steering the program off-track. Turnover in salespeople for many reasons is a reality for most sales organizations. Recruiting procedures for new salespeople must include an assessment of the candidate's fit to the organization's new sales culture.

To recap, the sales organization's assessment of the readiness of all the sale process participants to embrace adoption of the planned change is critical to the success of change adoption. This assessment must include all levels of people within the sales organization. Sales management may be called upon to make some hard personnel decisions prior to implementing the change based on this assessment. Once the change has been implemented the ability of all personnel to successfully adopt the new behavior must be monitored, and support provided to those who are struggling, or additional personnel decisions may be required. Sales force turnover is not unusual in sales organizations for several reasons. Management must therefore evaluate any new candidate's ability to perform in the new sales business process environment to avoid introducing inconsistent behaviors into their sales force.

2.6 Provide Coaching and Support for Adoption

Earlier it was described how both business value realization and successful change adoption are linked. A critical enabler in this equation is sales management coaching to drive the new desired behavior. Strong, consistent coaching by each sales manager can be utilized to overcome their salespeople's resistance to and fear of change, leading to adoption of the new CRM business system, and realization of the benefits/value expected by executive management. Successful change adoption through

> **Coaching** - "An ongoing and dynamic series of job-embedded interactions between a sales managers and direct report, designed to diagnose, correct, and reinforce behaviors specific to that individual". Source - Dixon and Adamson[14]

effective coaching is a leading indicator to benefits realization. If management waits for several months to determine if the expected business value is materializing it may be too late to take corrective action. To avoid this, sales management should periodically ask two questions following implementation of their new CRM business system to monitor the fulfillment their expectations:

- Initially, "Am I getting the expected behaviors?", and
- "Am I getting the expected business results (value)?"

Coaching is characterized as:

- Ongoing
- Customized – involves diagnose and corrective action specific to individual salesperson
- Behavioral – it's about demonstrating the application of skill and knowledge acquired through training
- Highly structured and regularly scheduled

Successful coaching drives salesperson change adoption which is a leading indicator of success in harvesting CRM business system benefits. Coaching builds and reinforces the sales culture that management envisioned. Coaching can be provided from two perspectives:

- *Process coaching* on the new business process and methodology where the focus is on "Why do I need to do this?" and "What do I do with the outcomes?"
- *Content coaching* on how to advance the sales opportunity including both the value of the data collected, and the opportunity strategy based upon the salesperson's assessment what was learned from this data.

Of the two types, in a sales organization with a mature, adopted, and effective CRM business system, content coaching is where the focus of coaching time should be spent.

Coaching is delivered primarily by the individual sales managers. But each may have different styles, personal understandings of or buy-in to the change, and personal adoption rates all of which can cause "message drift" resulting in inconsistencies in the adoption results achieved by each sales unit. To provide meaningful results the coaching messages must be consistently delivered across the entire sales organization. To minimize this drift, it is also essential to "coach the coaches" in order to keep all coaches focused on delivering the agreed upon key messages, in a consistent fashion, to their salespeople.

To be successful as the coaches' coach, the person performing this role (e.g., Chief Sales Business System Coach) must be seen as having the full empowerment

> A **Coach-of-Coaches** is required to ensure consistency of message across all sales manager coaches in the sales organization.

and sponsorship of the sales executives, have the respect of and acceptance by all sales managers to bring a mandatory change to their organization which they cannot duck, resist or impede, and be the source of knowledge on the change.

The sales managers should have sufficient confidence in this individual to feel open to discuss issues related to their personal concerns about and performance with the new business system. This chief coach role will coach and re-align where necessary these levels of sales management in both their coaching and conduct of the new CRM business process.

There is a large body of knowledge and experience that supports the premise that effective coaching is essential to change adoption. This is not up for discussion. Sales manager coaching enables the salespeople through the adoption period to a level where their new behavior in producing and using these outcomes becomes their new norm. Effective coaching can minimize the anticipated implementation dip and maximize adoption.

The question for sales executive management, raised by this book, is how do you know that the coaching is having the desired impact on achieving the adoption of the new business process? This adoption must be measured and managed as it ultimately drives the realization of the expected business benefits.

A very important partner with coaches in achieving the required change adoption is a *Help Desk support group*. As salespeople, managers, and others embrace the need to change their behavior with the new CRM business system they will ask three primary questions *"Why do I need to do this?"*, *"What do I do with the outcomes?"*, and *"How do I use the process and CRM tools to do this?"*

The support group people must be knowledgeable with the answers to all three, but their primary focus should be on supporting these sales users with the details of *"How"*, particularly as it gets closer to the technology interface, and thus clear any adoption obstacles related to the details of how to use the system. This in turn frees the coaches' time to work on the "Why" and "What" of adoption with the salespeople.

The role of this critical support group should include both responsive support to individual people, and also proactive action in identifying areas where salespeople are encountering problems, either individually or groups, and taking action to address same. Further, the group should also both report to sales management on success and failure of the salespeople, and collaborate with the "coach-of-coaches" on overall trends and recommended changes/enhancements to CRM business process and tools. The support group should leverage technology tools to facilitate communication with the users including company social web-sites, chat rooms, on-line chat capability, and other emerging technologies.

In summary, successful change adoption and business value realization are linked through successful coaching and support of all people who participate in the sales business process. A strong support group is essential to multiplying the effectiveness of the sales coaches in achieving adoption of the new CRM business process. All managers within the sales organization must perform in a coaching role. However, to maintain the consistency of the sales organization's message for change a "coach of coaches" role is also required. Having a strong, well supported, coaching program in place can lead to successful change adoption. The challenge for sales executives is to have the measurements in place to give them the visibility that the coaching efforts are having the desired impact on adoption of the new business process, which can enable their desired business benefits.

2.7 Measure Change Adoption Progress – A Critical Success Factor to Benefits Realization

The challenge with past implementations has been the lack of any kind of measurement of adoption of the new business process beyond anecdotal stories. Lacking a meaningful way to track the progress of change adoption puts the overall benefits of the CRM business system at great risk.

Salesperson adoption of the new business system comes from understanding and replicating the requisite new behavior. This is enabled with coaching assistance, until the desired level of proficiency with the new behavior is achieved. In order to make this progress observable and manageable, the new behavior must manifest itself in and be measurable through a few "high-gain" outcomes produced as a result of following the new sales business process.

These outcomes are both leading indicators of adoption, and critical input data to downstream sales process steps. Note: these outcomes must be observable, measureable results or deliverables; completed activities are not suitable as such outcomes! Metrics applied to such performance objects can be used to indicate progress toward successful behavior adoption.

> **Performance Metrics:** Measures used to both evaluate and improve the efficiency and effectiveness of the new sales business processes; as measured against a baseline established immediately prior to the implementation of the change.

Identifying these few "high-gain" outcomes will be a challenging exercise. For those organizations where a business case was initially developed to justify the CRM business system, assumptions about adoption should have been defined. During the development of that business case the sales leaders and managers who participated in the development of the results chain should have been asked to answer the question "What change is required to enable that outcome?", and then challenged with the follow up question "... and how will you know if your salespeople are adopting that change, specifically what few "hard" outcomes would you measure?" Their responses should have identified the basis for these few "high-gain" outcomes for their specific sales organization.

Those organizations looking to the experience of others to obtain a generic list of those few "high-gain" outcomes will unfortunately find, based on the research and feedback in discussions, that little has been published. While there is no consensus on specific outcomes, research and discussions for this book did reveal some common characteristics:

- There should only be a few (5 or less) selected from different stages in the organization's defined sales opportunity management process. Could include:
    - A single outcome if the organization has adopted a formal sales methodology, or,
    - Something more aggregated at the level of a key deliverable from a particular stage in the sales opportunity management process if no formal sales methodology is in place.
- The outcome, or deliverable should have measurable characteristics of:
    - Quality (a measure that is relevant to and adds value to the adoption of change).
    - Reusability in next steps in sales process.
- Sales manager coaching time on the outcome should be measurable.
- Highly desirable that data for the metric be captured as a by-product product of salesperson or sales manager activity, not an additional imposed task – the later will fail as salespeople in particular are reluctant to take the extra time to enter data that they see as used to just monitor or manage them.

As part of change adoption it is very important that everyone responsible for achieving a personal level of adoption be cognizant of these few "high-gain" outcomes, know the outcomes' contribution to sales opportunity success, and be able to identify effective actions based upon their understanding of the specific outcome. Producing quality outcomes can also provide management the means by which to evaluate individual sales manager and salesperson performance.

The following are examples of outcomes that could indicate progress in the adoption of change that leads to benefits realization. These surfaced as a result of research and on-line discussions:

- *Based on Sales Organization's Star Sales Performers Outcomes:* What does the sales behavior of the stars within the organization tell management about successful sales behavior? Can management distill this down to a few key outcomes or deliverables that indicate sales success? Can this be included in their change program as it is rolled out to all their salespeople?

- *Based on a Specific Validated Outcome:* This point is illustrated by the following two examples:
    1. Identification of one or more Strategic Client Coaches for the specific sales opportunity. Strategic Coaches are described by Miller-Heiman[15] as individuals in the client organization who can act as a guide for the opportunity, and who want your organization's solution at the exclusion of all others. This outcome has been validated by Miller-Heiman's research which found that engaging client coaches was a leading indicator for sales success.
    2. In the event that account planning actions are tracked through the new CRM, and specific client executives have been identified with which to establish a relationship the accomplishment of this

action (the outcome) could be such a measurable outcome.

- *Based on an Aggregated Outcome* (or otherwise called a deliverable): The following two examples, described by Miller-Heiman in their 2012 Sales Best Practices Study[5], illustrate an aggregated outcome:

    1. Identification of a qualified sales opportunity. Salespeople and sales managers are often in a hurry and often skip phases or stages in their sales process.

        For example, a RFP comes in the door; the salesperson and manager are a bit hungry; they quickly review the RFP and then conclude "Let's get a proposal in front of the client". The sales manager approves the allocation of proposal center and other scarce resources to the effort. The proposal is produced (in record time), submitted to the client. Then, 150 days later after the salesperson has failed to obtain a commitment or to otherwise validate client interest in buying, this opportunity is cancelled from the salesperson's pipeline.

        While there are good reasons to do this under certain circumstances, in general this is bad behavior! It is a waste of time and scarce resources, and might have directed critical resources away from an opportunity that would have had a chance of winning. The correct behavior would be to adequately qualify the opportunity up front before all these resources are allocated.

This qualification should be reviewed and approved by the sales manager and possibly others who would contribute resources to the pursuit. The measurable outcome would be – the sales manager has approved the sales opportunity as qualified. Further, the sales manager could include a quality rating of the qualification, for example: Strong, Average, Weak, or Failed.

- A strong qualification statement should include several specific pieces of known and evaluated information. These could include: an understanding of client prospect's issues and challenges in prospect's words; validation that sales organization has a viable solution to address these, confirmation that the Key Buyers and Influencers (i.e., Client Coaches) have need to buy, urgency to buy, means to buy, and finally, understanding/evaluating the sales organization's position in the client's buying process and the competitive landscape.

- Meaningful standards should be developed for each of these items to ensure consistency across the entire sales organization. These standards should be unambiguous and could provide the basis for an independent audit of conformity. Such an audit could be performed by a company's Internal Audit function, or an outside consulting organization.

2. Creation of a strong value statement that clearly ties the to-be proposed solution back to the prospective client's issues and challenges in specific qualified terms – sometimes referred to as the Business Case. The salesperson would prepare

and review this value statement with the Client Coach(es) and revise appropriately prior to submittal of any proposal. Further, it would also be reviewed and approved by the sales manager prior to submittal to client. The measurable outcome would be – the sales manager has approved the Value statement. As with the point above, the sales manager could include a quality rating of the value statement.

- *Based on Anecdotal/Subjective Evidence:* Some suggestions fell under the category of anecdotal/subjective evidence. These are good suggestions for collecting general trends but since they are not always unique to individuals they may not all that useful for identifying specific coachable behavior. They include:
    o Measuring the number of log-ins to the automated system. Sometimes challengeable by the nay-sayers who usually ask "How do you know that they logged in because they wanted to (new behavior), or they were told to (old behavior but with compliance to rules)? A more telling indicator is which salespeople are not logging in! Reporting the trend in logins can show that over time both a greater number of the salespeople and sales managers are logging in, and more frequently.
    o Call volume and call nature to Help Desk is another source – can provide more anecdotal stories about both the level of adoption and the nature of issues that salespeople and others are experiencing.
    o A meaningful measure for tracking change adoption could use a maturity scale that

incorporates the quality of the sales deliverable produced, usage of the deliverable in future steps, and how much one-on-one process coaching was required to produce the deliverable.

- o Use of "Like" and "Dislike" features on the CRM tool to focus on specific business process outcomes which salespeople concluded were or were not helpful in winning their deal.
- o Periodically use an on-line survey to measure sales force acceptance using a five point scale for measuring adoption of several key behaviors required by the new process.

For those organizations that choose not to make their chosen outcomes mandatory they could also add a measure of overall sales force adoption such as:

- Proportion of opportunities using the outcomes
- Proportion of the salespeople using the outcomes
- Perception of the usefulness of the outcomes by the salespeople (obtained through a survey, for example)

The most tangible of the "high-gain" outcomes described above are Specific Validated and Aggregated. These have the characteristics to which metrics can be applied. These outcomes are binary, either they were produced or not produced; if produced their quality can be assessed. They should be used in next steps, and they will initially require process coaching time to produce, all of which can be measured against a baseline to determine if change is occurring.

In the longer term, as these metrics indicate that change adoption is taking hold, sales executives will be able to measure the actual business performance of their CRM business process to track against their expected performance that was defined during the Vision Phase. These outcomes will differ for each organization according to its business issues and priorities. Patrick Seidell identified several generic process performance measures worth noting in a blog piece titled "5 Ways to Measure if Your Sales Process is Working"[16]. The following is a summary of Pat's key measures to use in gauging success of your sales process:

- Process Utilization: Are 90+% of your reps using the process? If so, this shows the process is delivering value for the sales team. The tools are useful and are helping them sell.

- Deal Size: Are average sales prices (or margins) increasing? This is a strong indication that your process is helping customers recognize needs. The process is enabling you to sell on value, not price.

- Forecast Accuracy: Is your pipeline-based forecast within 10% of reality? This is a great indicator that you are in step with the buyer. In addition, solid forecasting is a sign of consistent use of the process.

- Win Rates: Like deal size, win rates should improve in a measurable way. Your process is helping you beat the competition. Even if the competition is the status quo where the buyer takes no action.

- Sales Cycle Length: A good process will drive opportunities through the pipeline faster (*increased deal velocity*). It illustrates you haven't introduced friction and extra cycles into the process.

In addition to these consider adding the following measure:

- Deal Cancellation Rates: If the new sales business process has been adopted, deal cancellation rates, measured after the point in your process where deals are properly qualified, should be reduced significantly. High cancellation rates are a strong indicator that deals have been not properly qualified with the client, and that salespeople have rushed to get a proposal or bid in front of a customer who may have no sense of urgency, or need, or ability to buy. Reducing the number of unqualified deals both frees up sales time and resources to work on deals that have real buyers, and improves sales forecast accuracy by eliminating uncertain deals from what should be the high probability portion of the pipeline. However, if a deal that was evaluated as qualified was lost, this is an indication that something went wrong post qualification and the reason for this should be identified and addressed.

> **Idea:** A starting point for a sales organization could be to start tracking a single key "high-gain" outcome, then as tracking metrics indicate that adoption is taking hold, add a second, third, etc. As an example, start with the sales opportunity qualification, then as the metrics on this outcome indicates that adoption is taking place, add the value statement.

It is highly desirable that these chosen outcomes should be measureable as a result of "do-the-business" actions and not require an extraordinary effort. Sales executives should periodically have an audit conducted by an independent party, perhaps their internal audit group, to ensure that the outcomes are been held to the established standards. This would surface any instances of sales managers making short sighted "good enough" judgments that would compromise the entire program.

In summary, adoption of the changes brought by the new CRM business system results in new behavior by the sales force which ultimately enables the envisioned benefits of the business system. To achieve this adoption of new behavior by the salespersons, sales manager coaching is required. In order to manage both adoption and the efficacy of sales manager coaching, sales management must measure progress on salespersons' creation /use of identified key new "high-gain" sales business process outcomes which are leading indicators of success in winning the sales opportunity. Several examples of such outcomes have been described. Executive sales management must insist that a few be selected, that measurement on progress toward creating these or replacement outcomes occurs, and that appropriate actions are taken to achieve successful, lasting change adoption. Once adoption takes hold management should insist on measuring the overall performance of their sales process to ensure that is delivering their expected business benefits.

2.8 Evaluate the Role of Compensation in Achieving Change Adoption

Implementing change in sales business processes and technology generally impacts all participants across the sales organization. It is important that the organization's compensation plan motivates these people to adopt the new behavior demanded by the new business process.

In the past, organizations generally implemented change to process and systems, but continued to compensate salespeople and sales managers solely on making their quota numbers. The numbers were usually a stretch and after all the participants recovered from the "shock" of the new business process and technology they fall back to the immediate need (maybe even panic) of focusing on making their numbers, often setting aside the hard work of adopting the new behavior.

If an organization is to achieve the desired adoption of change the first line sales managers, in particular, must pay close attention to both coaching and leadership on the new business processes - working with their salespeople to coach them through adoption of the change to the new level of performance. Compensation should play a role in enabling change adoption. To recognize the significant role that these sales managers play in achieving change adoption consider splitting their compensation, say 50/50, between making their sales unit numbers and achieving measureable behavior change through effective coaching. Such a split could be maintained until the sales force is clearly demonstrating sustained performance at the new level of behavior.

This compensation topic received considerable discussion in a LinkedIn Discussion Group [*Does Sales Manager Compensation Play a Role in New CRM Adoption?*]; with some members favoring, and some wondering if it was necessary. Those who favored commented that putting compensation on the table for this change adoption effort would both put the right focus on achieving adoption, and fairly compensate the sales manager for change results delivered during a period when sales volume might dip. A concern expressed was the potential for sending the wrong message. That is, if the salespeople's' perception was that the sales manager spent their day doing what they defined as "coaching" with no measurable business results, the overall optics could be negative. In order to deal with this reasonable concern it would be important to measure the effectiveness of the sales manager's coaching efforts in achieving measureable change adoption by their individual salespeople. In this approach the sales manager receives compensation during this change period for sales made by sales team, and for repositioning sales team's selling behavior to enable higher levels of sales performance.

Any compensation considerations could be driven by the principle that "People generally do what they get paid to do." Those designing the compensation system would need to work closely with those planning the business change both to identify the specific, measureable required new behavior, and to design a compensation structure that would reward achievement of the new behavior. Some examples the designers could choose include:

- Sales manager's effectiveness both in coaching, and repositioning the manager's sales team members to the desired change in behavior.

- Salesperson's proficiency in producing quality business outcomes as they move their opportunities through the sales business process.

- Lowering sales quotas at all levels within the sales organization structure (i.e., salesperson to sales executive) during the period of maximum change adoption (e.g., the implementation dip), in recognition of the extra burden of adopting the new business process and technology.

> **Note:** A more successful compensation plan will be best planned with coordination between business change planners and compensation planners, and focused on driving the desired sales force behavior.

In summary, each organization planning a CRM business system implementation will have to deal with sales management engagement, salesperson engagement, while generating vigorous support for change adoption, all occurring over an extended period of time. Sales management, in particular the first line managers, are the critical players in embedding this change. This speaks to the need for sales executives to evaluate including sales manager compensation (and salesperson compensation) as motivation for achieving this desired behavior change within their broader vision and plan.

2.9 Implement Overall Program Governance – *Pulling It All Together*

The lessons learned from past CRM business system implementations showed that the efforts were too narrowly focused on the implementation of the technical solution, and beyond "go-live" the efforts quickly became "orphans" with little or no on-going

> **Program governance** of a CRM business system is a cradle-to-grave effort, with initial focus on system implementation and adoption, followed by continuous improvement.

senior sales management care and feeding. Sales organizations must exercise strong program governance over the entire life of their CRM business system business system in order to successfully realize their goals for its implementation. This governance includes the leadership and sponsorship that both authorizes and legitimizes the pending change.

Salespeople will also look to this governance to evaluate the company's commitment to the change. This is very important as salespeople need to have confidence that their sales executives are committed to making the change happen. Program governance must cover three key aspects of their CRM business systems' life.

- Initially, the dual challenges of project management of the CRM business solution's successful turn-over, and the people-side of change adoption, then
- The longer term management of its on-going operation for continuous improvement.

This governance, led by the sales executives, should include:

- Aligned, active support and sponsorship by senior management (sales executives).
- Clearly identify all critical stakeholders across all business units and affected functions.
- Facilitate agreement around success criteria for all affected.
- Clearly communicated expectations for all participants across the affected functions.
- Approval and guidance of all program initiatives including program updates and re-prioritizations.
- Actively monitor progress toward change adoption success, adjust when necessary.

- Manage the realization of the expected benefits of the program.
- On-going, periodic evaluation of the CRM business system's performance, with approval for any business system changes to further enhance performance.

Identifying the sales organization 'Change Sponsor' of the people-side program, and identifying relevant benefit owners with assigned responsibility for realizing individual benefits envisioned in the program's benefits plan (all of whom are aware of their roles throughout this program) can ensure full benefits realization.

> **Change Sponsor:** a senior sales executive formally assigned the responsibility, authority and accountability for realization of the CRM business system program benefits.

This should include some very real reward or consequence (such as a major impact to their compensation) for hitting or missing the envisioned benefits for the CRM business system investment. The sponsor and benefits owners will deliver to the program helpful input, suitable measures, and most importantly, adequate buy-in and support to achieve defined success. This sponsorship and accountability has been shown to be the "missing ingredient" in many CRM implementations. This is where the change in behavior must start.

To realize the full potential of the CRM business system's lifetime benefits, senior sales management must be accountable for getting the adoption of the change required (both business and technology) to realize the initial envisioned benefits, and for further benefits resulting from continuous improvement. Fujitsu's Macroscope defines this as activist accountability which goes beyond traditional notions of passive accountability. It includes the concept of "ownership" - meaning active, continuous engagement in:

- The management process to achieve the intended business result and the associated benefits.
- Managing a program with clear ownership of outcomes and the associated benefits.

Benefits realization must be an on-going effort driven by the change sponsor who has accepted responsibility for achieving the expected value of this new CRM business system, and who is actively engaged in discharging same. Key events both during implementation and then in production should include:

- Establish baseline measures for the specific benefit outcomes identified in the Benefits Plan (these outcomes discussed in "2.7 Measure Change Adoption Progress"
- Ensure the capability to report on the measures are included in the design/build of the business solution;
- Look for other change-outcome opportunities that were not initially envisioned but emerge and have potential to enhance benefits. This could include something overlooked, or a change that could create meaningful value.
- Conduct formal value realization reviews at the six month point following implementation, and then annually to follow that, continue tracking measures, and implementing change that drives value on an on-going basis. Both the formal reviews and the on-going tracking could yield initiatives to correct behaviors that were not leading to the value outcomes.

In summary, program management enables the realization of the benefits of a CRM business system implementation. It pulls together implementation as well as both change program management and benefits management which must go hand-in-hand. Sales executive management must identify a change sponsor with activist accountability. The change sponsor must establish a formal benefits review schedule to report on progress toward benefits realization and to take any required corrective or enhancement action. Successful program management goes on for the life of the business system.

3. FRAMEWORK FOR HARVESTING CRM VALUE

Pulling It All Together

The previous sections discussed several ingredients to success. This section describes when in the life-cycle of the business system these ingredients need to be considered. To guide the transition from bright idea to realized benefits, the four phase life-cycle framework, illustrated in figure 3.1 below, can be used:

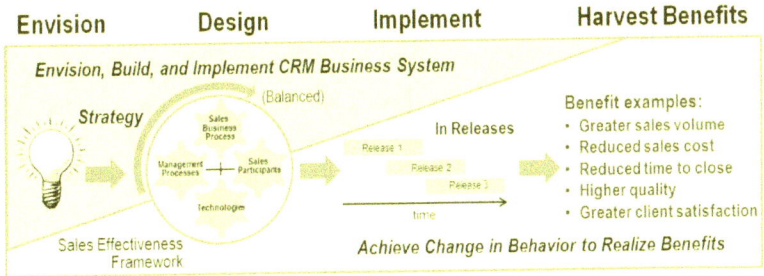

Figure 3.1 CRM Benefits Realization Framework

The flow through each phase of the framework is generally left to right. The amount of time required to accomplish the deliverables of each phase is not represented by the diagram. The Harvest Benefits phase should continue through to the end of business solution's life.

The purpose of each Phase is:

1. *Vision for CRM – Start with Right Perspective, and Right People!*
    - Purpose: to enable sales management (all levels including executive) and other key stakeholders to express their vision of their new CRM business system in clear and unambiguous business terms. This phase includes defining the business value of the envisioned business system, and how this value will be delivered.

2. *Design*
    - Purpose: to complete the design of the CRM business system envisioned by sales management and other stakeholders in the Envision Phase.

3. *Implement*
    - Purpose: to implement the CRM business system as designed in the Design Phase. Depending upon the Implementation Plan this may be done in several releases of designed business functionality. This phase ends when the sales organization has formally "accepted" the CRM business system.

4. *Harvest the Benefits*
    - Purpose: to achieve full adoption of the business change, and harvest the resulting initial benefits defined in Envision Phase, and over time, as the business system is in operation, those benefits resulting from continuous improvement.

As noted earlier, there are two required but different efforts involved

1. Envision, build and implement the solution – the traditional CRM Project, with a defined start and end date and a formal project structure and team, with the objective of obtaining sales management acceptance of the implemented business system.

2. Achieve the adoption of the change in salespersons' behavior, i.e. people-side, required by the new CRM business system in order to realize its envisioned benefits. This is operational in nature and the focus is to continually manage the business operation to achieve the business goals and objectives for the

business system defined by executive management initially during the Envision phase and updated during the life of the business.

This chapter focuses on the later effort (as the first is generally well known), and describes the *key outcomes* which can contribute to achieving the adoption of the change in behavior of the new CRM business system. (Outcomes are so much more observable and measureable than activities!) Its content includes the thinking of others including John Kenney Sr. Consultant at Sales Benchmark Index [17], and Jason Whitehead CEO of Tri-Turns [18]. For ease of reading these major outcomes/deliverables are presented in point form.

Adoption is achieved in "Digestible" Chunks: For simplicity this book presents design, implement, and adoption as a set of serial events. However, in reality, to avoid overwhelming all participants with a large amount of change, implementation is normally conducted in releases of change. Adults learn by doing. A common approach is to introduce an increment of change that can be mastered within a two to three month period, then introduce a second, third, etc. until the majority of the change that will contribute to overall value has been introduced and adopted. The order of change increments should be based on its contribution to value. After the second or third increment of change, pause the change introduction for a period of time to allow the accumulated change to become mastered, and to avoid change fatigue.

3.1 Vision for CRM – Start with Right Perspective, and Right People!

The following will be accomplished during the Vision phase:

- The new CRM business system Governance Group is established. Initially its focus will be on envisioning and designing the new business system, later transitioning to operationalizing the system to achieve adoption of the new behavior and to harvest the envisioned benefits. There are three key roles in this group:
    - *Executive Change Sponsor* – usually the chief sales officer.
    - *Benefit Owners* – those responsible for specific benefits within the sales organization.
    - *Chief Sales Coach* (AKA Coach-of-coaches, or Chief Sales Business System Coach) – this role is responsible for ensuring that the new CRM business process is operationalized according to the approved design and consistently applied across all units of the sales organization. In some organizations this role could be performed by the Sales Operations Manager. In some situations this role could be performed by an outside consultant, particularly if the sales organization has also decided to implement a formal sales methodology.

  In addition, to support the change sponsor with the change adoption program, add change management competence to the people-side adoption effort.

- A vision of how the new CRM business system supports the goals and objectives of the sales organization has been created. In part it defines the sales culture that executive management sees as driving the required new sales behavior. This culture defines those things which executive management see of value and enables a set of shared mental assumptions within the sales organization that guide their day-to-day interpretation and action in the sales organization.

- The benefits of the envisioned CRM business system have been identified in the results chain and linked with assumptions about required sales behavior changes. The benefits vision must include visibility to two key items:
  - The implementation dip immediately following "go-live"
  - The percentage of overall benefits tied to salespeople adoption of the requisite change

  Initial outcomes that can be used to measure/track the progress of this changed behavior have been identified.

- The strategy for change adoption and reinforcement for the new CRM business system has been defined. The strategy includes a description of the approach which sales executive management will use, along with the necessary resources, to achieve the required adoption of new sales behavior necessary to enable the envisioned benefits. This strategy should include:
  - On-going measurement and reporting of metrics about several key outcomes that indicate progress on the required change in behavior of the sales force that will enable the envisioned benefits. There must be compliance around this reporting as on-going monitoring and management of change behavior action at all levels will be critical to successful change adoption.

- A way for participants in the sales organization to contribute ideas to the new CRM business system. People generally adopt things that they have had some input into; and salespeople generally have great examples about what is both good and bad about the current operation.
- Sales executives' position on the role of compensation in achieving change adoption. Candidate areas were described in the section on Compensation.

- Change communication plans have been developed, and, at a minimum, the following two communications have been issued to all impacted people in the new CRM business system:
  - The first communication should occur at the kick-off of the Envision Phase; its content should include the business reasons for the undertaking (what issues/problems are being addressed) what sales executive expects to accomplish and how, who will be involved and impacted, what is the expected timeline, a way for participants in the sales organization to contribute ideas to the new business system, and what is expected business-as-usual behavior for the sales organization during this time.
  - The final communication should occur immediately following the end of the Envision Phase. Its content should include a description of the vision for the new CRM business system, the benefits expected, the expected changes in sales behavior required by the sales organization to achieve these benefits, and the major phases of the plan to go from vision to harvest benefits.

3.2 Design

The following will be accomplished during the Design phase of the program:

- Benefits of the envisioned CRM business system have been linked to assumptions about required changes in sales force behavior have been revised and recorded in the results chain. Expected benefits have been associated with which people in the sales organization must adopt and use the new CRM system. Key measures of change adoption have been identified for these changed behavior assumptions, and standards established for each.

- Sales organization structure, support, and role decisions that are required to support successful change adoption have been made.

- Change Assessment has been conducted based on the gap between the current business system and the new business system. Assessment identifies the early adopters and late adopters. Includes in-depth assessment of the sales managers' capabilities for change and coaching. Senior management should be prepared to make some personnel decisions based on this assessment.

- A change adoption and reinforcement plan has been developed, with:
    - Guidelines to support sales manager coaching given to training material development team. To include:
        - What is to be measured
        - What represents good vs. bad measures; implications of each are described
        - How often to review with their "coaches"

- Approach to ensuring consistent coaching across all sales managers and sales units developed. Chief Coach to have key role in executing this approach.

- Report requirements for sales management tracking of adoption of and compliance with new behavior are provided to development team. Tracking of compliance and mastery at all levels within the sales organization will be critical to successful change adoption. Reports to provide views of compliance and mastery at several levels including sales manager view of each salesperson; view of each sales manager, view of each sales division, etc. This reporting to include visibility to each person in the sales organization who was expected to produce which benefit. Reports to include changes from baseline measures, and from previous period.

- User Acceptance Survey defined and provided to development team for development of on-line survey. Survey tool to be used in periodic assessment of user satisfaction and acceptance of new CRM business system.

- Benefits management within the governance plan identified. The specific metrics that sales executives will use to measure the actual performance of their CRM business process against their expected outcomes are defined. Examples of expected outcomes include: increased sales volume, increased deal size, improved win rates, reduced cost of sales, reduced elapsed time in sales cycle from initial lead to signed contract, and improved customer satisfaction.

- A plan for periodic independent audit of the reported results has been developed.

- Plans for using compensation in achieving change adoption finalized, including recognizing and rewarding those who demonstrate mastery of the new CRM business process and tools behaviors, and for those who take a leadership role in promoting change to the new behavior.
- CRM business system implementation plans finalized. Note: depending upon the assessed amount of business change plans may include implementing system functionality in releases.
- Change Communication has occurred focused in more detail on:
  - How new system will impact each participant.
    - How the change in new behavior will be measured, as well as acceptable standards for the new adopted behavior.
    - Plans for training all participants.
    - Statement by sales executives that it is the personal responsibility of all sales participants (salespeople and managers all levels) to develop the expected level of mastery of the new CRM business process and tools for their role.
    - Plans for implementation and on-going support.
    - Introduction of rewards program for recognizing those who demonstrate mastery of the new behavior, and for those who take a leadership role in promoting change to the new behavior.
- Plans for selection, induction, orientation, and training of new hire sales participants have been developed. Plan ensures that new hires are selected for their "fit" for the

culture of the sales organization that executive sales management is working to create and strengthen. Upon entry they are brought into the new culture.

3.3 Implement

The following will be accomplished during the Implement phase of the program:

- Governance body focus and membership has been revised. Focus of Governance now on implementing, achieving adoption of new business system, and harvesting CRM business system benefits. Includes operationalizing, managing continuous improvement based on change adoption measures to achieve expected benefits, and approval of additional initiatives required to achieve expected benefits.

- Training for initial capabilities developed and delivered, recorded, and available on demand (web based). All training sessions to be made available on demand to all users who miss a session, or who need reinforcement training. Initial participant training is on released functionality of both business process (with business rules) and technical infrastructure. Training for sales managers includes areas of:
    - Business process and automated functionality
    - Understanding the adoption outcomes
    - Implications of business process changes on nature of sales pipeline
    - Using the change adoption tracking reports

- o Effective coaching
- o Mastery and Compliance assessment and reporting

- Sales user support plan developed. A strong sales user support group, e.g., Help Desk, is critical to successful and consistent change adoption. Plan defines strong support capability of how users and coaches will be supported in "using" the new business system following "Go-Live".

- Updated change adoption and reinforcement plan available, based on what is learned during Implement Phase.

- Change Communication has occurred including:
  - o Reaction to and lessons learned for initial training implementation.
  - o Plans for additional more in-depth training on existing or new functionality.
  - o Reminder that sales executives believe that it is the personal responsibility of all sales participants (salespeople and managers all levels) to develop the level of mastery of the new CRM business process and tools expected for their role.
  - o User support capability available.
  - o Tips/suggestions on how to master the new behavior and system capabilities.
  - o Reminder of rewards program for recognizing those who demonstrate mastery of the new behavior, and for those who take a leadership role in promoting change to the new behavior.

3.4 Harvest the Benefits

This stage ensures that the CRM business system is operationalized as envisioned and that through continuous improvement the new behavior is adopted, and that its benefits are realized and enhanced over the life of the business system. This stage includes the following major on-going activities or events that will lead toward the expected benefits of the CRM business system implementation. Keep in mind that while this section is focused on achieving change adoption, it is also important to remember that in parallel with these change activities the business of winning sales deals must also go on.

- Sales User Training and Support:
    o Sales User Support available on-demand (focused on "how-to" issues and questions, and providing critical feedback on successes and failures of users as well as recommended changes/enhancements to enable greater adoption).
    o On-going new capability and reinforcement training:
        - Live session (one hour) for new functionality.
        - All training sessions recorded, and available on demand (web based) to all users who missed a session, or who need reinforcement training.
- Achieving Change Adoption at Sales Unit Level:
    o Salesperson coaching and reinforcement sessions - focused on diagnostic and corrective actions to assist salesperson master the behavior of the new business process, methods, and techniques. Lead by sales manager, may periodically include support of others (e.g., Chief Sales Coach) with expertise in areas

pertinent to session. Sales manager observes and coaches to both assist salesperson in developing mastery in following the sales process as well as producing the prescribed key deliverables within each stage. Good practice in support of coaching is for sales manager and salesperson(s) to work on live deals using the CRM business process and tools. Can be conducted:

- Weekly one-on-one for first three months following go-live, can shift to biweekly for next six month period depending upon salesperson's adoption of change. These meetings are critical to change adoption. The repetition in coaching and use of business process can lead to mastery in both sales manager and salesperson. Note: There may be a tendency to abandon these meetings early, or skip a few, but to do so can put successful change adoption at risk.
- "On the spot" coaching as required. This is very effective for quick direction topics, more lengthy discussion should be referred to the weekly meeting.

o Bi-weekly sales team group sessions to conduct a deep dive into a specific area of new functionality or an area where all users are experiencing difficulty (e.g., moving an opportunity through a certain Stage in the opportunity management process). The key point here is – use this format when a topic applies to all users. Covering a topic of interest to only some within the group while efficient for the sales managers will be seen as a waste of time by the other users. Led by sales manager, may periodically include support of others with expertise in areas pertinent to session.

- Sales manager preparation for each weekly session includes: information from the CRM business system showing the salespersons' change adoption metrics, the number of connections the salesperson has made with the CRM, and observations by the sales manager and feedback provided from others including the user support group, clients, and other company participants in the sales business process.

- Sales manager conducts "Ride along" sessions with each salesperson by meeting with clients to observe the salesperson's use of the business process, methods, tools, techniques, technical infrastructure. Diagnostic and reinforcement feedback to be provided at the end of each session. As a guideline sales managers should conduct this session 3 to 6 times with each salesperson within first 6 to 9 months of "Go-Live".

- Sales manager assessment report of change adoption. Sales manager to record assessment of each salesperson's level of mastery and compliance with the CRM business process and tools. Would be done bi-weekly initially and as level of mastery and compliance grows could be moved to monthly.

- Sales executive calls to a salesperson to discuss details of a specific sales opportunity are seen as an effective way to reinforce adoption and engagement.

• Driving Consistent Change Adoption Across Sales Organization:
  - Chief Sales Coach to report to sales executive and sales management team on accuracy and consistency of CRM business system adoption across the sales organization.

- Cross sales manager coaching to minimize "message drift" purpose includes:
  - "Sitting-in" on and providing direction when necessary to:
    - Sales manager one-on-one sessions, and group sessions
    - Sales division sessions
  - Working with sales manager to align message, input includes observations for change adoption measurements, observations from salesperson coaching sessions, sales division coaching session, feedback from others.
  - Working with sales management levels above sales unit managers to bring ensure consistency.

- Communicating Change Adoption and Reinforcement:
  - Regular email status update from sales management (weekly or biweekly) focused on roll-out news, success stories, change adoption, featured capabilities
  - Sales Executive Leadership Calls (biweekly during first quarter) focused on importance of new CRM business system, recognition of both success stories and people who "get it", update on progress of change adoption, reminder of adoption incentives.

- Achieving Change Adoption and Realizing Envisioned Benefits – driven by Change Sponsor:
  - Sales managers (first line up to sales executives) monthly, quarterly and semiannual progress reviews on change adoption and realization of benefits. Input includes change measurements, compliance and mastery measures, and sales performance both against

benchmarks, with trends over previous period, User Acceptance Survey, and feedback from others. Each manager analyzes results and corrective action is taken. Each manager reviews results of same with their manager.

- Governance group, led by Change Sponsor, reviews quarterly, semiannual, and annual progress, and takes corrective action. Reviews to include two types of progress toward harvesting the benefits of the new CRM business system:
  - "Are we getting the adoption of expected behaviors?" - Report on adoption progress. How has the level of mastery and compliance changed since beginning and last report?
  - "Are we getting the expected business results from the new CRM business system?" - Benchmark the performance of the new CRM business system. Metrics to be used including the specific objectives and success criteria set by sales management in the Envision Phase. Several generic measures were described earlier in Section 2.7 Measure Change Adoption Progress.
  - Both of these should yield insights on recommended periodic corrective, reinforcement, and advancement initiatives going forward.

- Reporting on periodic audits of reported results by an independent source to ensure results are reported against standards consistency across entire organization, as ordered by the Governance group. If necessary plans of action developed and initiated as result of these audits.

- Induction orientation and training of new sales participants. New hires are screened and selected for their "fit" to the culture of the sales organization that executive sales management is working to create and strengthen, and upon entry are brought into the culture.

As noted in the introductory paragraph of this section, in addition to the above, keep in mind that the following actions are on-going in parallel with the change adoption program and *intended to focus on winning sales*, but do have change adoption implications:

- Sales manager's weekly cadence call with direct report salespeople to review sales opportunities in their pipelines, using the CRM tools. Sales manager observations about a specific salesperson's approach or pipeline content can be great input into a coaching session.

- Sales Opportunity Strategy Sessions where sales manager and salesperson meet collaboratively to both creatively identify why an opportunity has lost traction, and to identify creative ways to advance it with prospective customer. These sessions occur as required and use the new CRM business process, tools and techniques. Lessons learned in these sessions become great input to other strategy sessions or group operational or adoption calls.

SUMMARY

Once the formal assigned CRM project team has implemented the new CRM business system, and successfully obtained user sign-off, they generally pack up and move on to their next assignment, leaving the sales organization solely with the responsibility for both adopting the change required by the new business system, and harvesting it's envisioned benefits. This is a daunting task, one for which many are generally neither expecting, nor prepared. Consequently, to realize the business benefits of their CRM business system implementation, sales executives must engage, prepare their organization, and lead it through the successful change in behavior that will enable their expected business benefits.

Sales management at all levels within the organization are responsible for the full adoption, by all salespeople, that will enable the harvesting of benefits of the new CRM business system. This starts with sales executive's defining the vision of the new CRM business system which often involves a change in sales behavior that enables their expected benefits. During the Envision Phase of the approach described in this book, sales executives start by clearly defining their stated goals and objectives for the new CRM business system, and end with a clear understanding of the business change adoption by salespeople that is required to meet same. This understanding of the amount of change can assist sales management in their assessment of each and all salespeople's' likelihood of meeting the challenge of full adoption, and over what time period.

The change management effort to realize the CRM system benefits is sales organization-wide. Sales management, in particular first line sales managers are critical to driving adoption in the Harvest Benefits phase. Sales managers coach their salespeople on the new CRM business system to overcome resistance and fear. They coach for process adoption; for content on a particular sales opportunity, and they bring innovative approaches required to advance sales opportunities. Sales executives reinforce the vision, identify and reward new levels of adoption, and provide the time and resources for the sales managers and other salespeople to successfully adopt the new CRM business system. The sales executive change sponsor and the chief coach are responsible for consistent roll out across their sales organization.

Tracking successful change adoption is critical to realizing the business benefits. The challenge for sales executives is to have measurements in place that will provide them with evidence that coaching efforts are leading to adoption of the new business process. Full adoption by all people who participate in the sales business process enables the specific benefits that sales executives identified, and allows them to meet their goals for their CRM business system. Executive sales management must insist that a few measures be selected, that measurement on progress toward creating these or replacement outcomes occurs, and that appropriate actions are taken to achieve successful, lasting change adoption. Once adoption takes hold, management should insist on measuring the overall business results performance of their sales process to ensure that is delivering their expected business benefits.

In addition to achieving their immediate sales process improvement goals, sales executives will have also positioned their organization for an additional strategic benefit flowing from the organization learning that it has just acquired. This learning will enable this organization to absorb future business change with greater ease, in a shorter period of time providing a significant competitive advantage over other sales organizations who are struggling with change implementation.

This sounds daunting, particularly with all the pressure for immediate sales performance. But, this is what great leaders do. In the "middle of the swamp" they find a way build infrastructure and develop organization capability to ensure future success and growth.

SOURCES:

1. CRM failure rates: 2001-2009   Michael Krigsman   August, 2009 http://www.zdnet.com/blog/projectfailures/crm-failure-rates-2001-2009/4967

2. " Avoid the CRM Failure Zone: Five Steps to Achieving Success" by Tri Tuns eBook series on CRM effectiveness www.TriTuns.com

3. "63% of CRM Initiatives Fail - CRM initiatives currently have a 63% fail rate, according to a new study by Merkle Group Inc. The CRM firm surveyed 352 senior-level, U.S.-based executives in $1+ billion organizations regarding their company's CRM initiatives and their attitudes about those initiatives." By Jonathan Prezant July 17, 2013 Direct Marketing News. http://www.merkleinc.com/thought-leadership/feature-articles/2013/63-crm-initiatives-fail

4. "According to a study conducted by McKinsey & Company, nearly 75% of new sales process implementations are not adopted by the sales force." From Why Do Good Reps Resist Sales Process Improvement? By John Kenney on Tue, May 08, 2012 http://www.salesbenchmarkindex.com/bid/83152/Why-Do-Good-Reps-Resist-Sales-Process-Improvement

5. The Miller Heiman Research Institute's 2012 Executive Summary of Miller Heiman Sales Best Practices Study http://www.millerheiman.com/Knowledge_Center/Knowledge_Center_Articles/Sales_Performance_Research/2012_Executive_Summary_of_Miller_Heiman_Sales_Best/

6. Twenty-five percent of global organizations reveal CRM as their top spending priority for the next two years, while interest continues to grow in cloud services and mobile. Gartner User Survey Analysis: CRM, Cloud and Mobile Dominate Application Software Spending Trends March 2013   https://www.gartner.com/doc/2360716

Sources

7. "With 70 to 80 percent ..." Miller Heiman Sales Performance Journal: The True Test of Sales Strategy [Q2.2013] - http://www.millerheiman.com/Knowledge_Center/Knowledge_Center_Articles/Sales_Performance_Journal/Journal-The-True-Test-of-Sales-Strategy/

8. Donald A. Marchand and Joe Peppard - DESIGNED TO FAIL: WHY IT PROJECTS UNDERACHIEVE AND WHAT TO DO ABOUT IT http://www.som.cranfield.ac.uk/som/dinamic-content/media/ISRC/Designed%20to%20Fail%20Working%20Paper.pdf

9. Fujitsu Macroscope – Benefits Realization http://macroscope.ca.fujitsu.com/Products/benefits-realization.html

10. Managing the Realization of Business Benefits from IT Investments Professor Joe Peppard Cranfield School of Management, et al http://www.som.cranfield.ac.uk/som/dinamic-content/research/documents/peppardwarddaniel07.pdf

11. Change Management – Wikipedia http://www.scribd.com/doc/141925583/Change-Management-Wikipedia-The-Free-Encyclopedia

12. Change Management Learning Center - Prosci "ROI of Change Management *People Side Benefit Contribution*", http://www.change-management.com/tutorial-roi-of-cm-mod1.htm

13. "Some sales research organizations indicate that a very small percentage of sales training provides any lasting increase in sales volume." Jacques Werth, MBA http://www.linkedin.com/groups/Some-sales-resarch-organizations-indicate-78609.S.268753951?qid=5aa33fa2-4462-449e-b2d4-44e87a66524e&trk=groups_search_item_list-0-b-ttl

14. *The Challenger Sale* Matthew Dixon and Brent Adamson Published by Penguin Group 2011
    http://www.executiveboard.com/exbd-resources/content/challenger/index.html

15. Strategic Selling® - Miller Heiman
    http://www.millerheiman.com/Our_Products/Strategic_Selling/

16. "5 Ways to Measure if Your Sales Process is Working" Patrick Seidell Sales & Marketing Effectiveness Blog
    http://www.salesbenchmarkindex.com/bid/97242/5-Ways-to-Measure-if-Your-Sales-Process-is-Working

17. Autopsy of a Failed Sales Process Implementation John Kenney, May, 2012
    http://www.salesbenchmarkindex.com/bid/83784/Autopsy-of-a-Failed-Sales-Process-Implementation

18. "Avoid the CRM Failure Zone: Five Steps to Achieving Success" Tri Tuns' eBook Jason Whitehead CEO
    http://www.trituns.com/SPECIAL/eBook1_registration.html

ABOUT THE AUTHOR

Dean Sharratt is a successful management consultant and sales professional focusing on assisting business organizations to improve the effectiveness of their sales function. Out of his experience and research came a focus on better understanding what contributes to successful adoption of change in sales business processes. This led to Dean writing this book.

Dean's relevant experience includes:

- Past 10 years focused on sales business process implementation/improvement, sales reporting and dashboards, sales methodologies and techniques, CRM selection, Salesforce.com implementation/evolution, and implementing organizational change;
- Prior to that, many years of significant, successful experience in both direct sales of large, complex solutions, and in managing an IT services consulting business.

www.ingramcontent.com/pod-product-compliance
Lightning Source LLC
Chambersburg PA
CBHW051727170526
45167CB00002B/830